HOW TO SEPARATE YOURSELF

IBRAHIM KAMARA
UNCLE SKOOB

FOREWORD

We must be 100% brutally honest with ourselves and those around us to really reach our full potential. The truth hurts. We all know it. While lies bring comfort, the comfort is very short-lived in the grand scheme of life. While the damage is more so permanent. The results of this false comfort are extremely detrimental, compared to the temporary pain that we would experience from actually embracing the truth. Enduring the pain that we experience while embracing the reality of our current situation only makes us stronger in the long run. Compared to when we are not honest with ourselves, and we rob ourselves of the opportunity for real growth. How can we advance in any area of life without being completely honest of where we are right now in that area? We cannot. We can only advance to the fullest by being completely transparent, aware, and honest with ourselves about where we currently stand. We can then begin marking our progress based on the improvements from our previous condition. As we continue to get better our confidence in our abilities will continue to grow. However, we must trust and see the process to the end, to reap the full results and benefits we seek. This process is the only thing standing before you and your wildest dreams. How beautiful is it to realize that you are literally the only thing standing before you and all that your heart desires?

DEDICATION

This book is dedicated to all dreamers who are soon to become do-ers. This book is not a philosophical book based on a bunch of abstract ideas or complex concepts that are difficult to grasp. Rather, this book contains simple practical steps, designed to help you reach your full potential. It does not matter what you have deemed your dream, purpose or mission is on this earth. You can apply this knowledge through these 6 steps on your journey to becoming the best version of yourself, accomplishing your goals, fulfilling your purpose, and living out your dreams.

INSTRUCTION

There are interactive sections of this book, where you are asked to answer a few questions after reading a section. It is important that you honestly brainstorm and answer these questions. Purchasing this book is a great step in the right direction, but we all have fallen victim to buying a book and not actually applying the information in the book. It may end up in our hands because we borrow it from a trusted friend, or we buy it because it is a best seller, etc. It does not matter how we get the book, just as it does not matter if we read the book. What matters is if we actually apply the information in the book. That is the whole purpose of me writing this book. While I do feel I am a funny guy, this is not for entertainment! It is for enlightenment. If you are reading or looking for entertainment, I will have something for you soon as well. There is nothing wrong with entertainment, but there is a time and place for everything. The 6 steps in this book are sequential and can be repeated and mastered until your goal has been met.

Carefully reading this book and most importantly, answering these questions after you have read each section will allow you to open your eyes and clearly see what adjustments you need to make, in your personal life. So that you can actually accomplish your true goals. You have to really know yourself to even know your true goals. Discovering your real self in this sense is a process alone which we are going to help you with.

PREFACE

A lot of the so called goals and dreams we spend our lives going after, are ones that have been projected onto us by someone other than ourselves. These other people are usually our loved ones who actually have our best interest at heart.

One example would be going to college to satisfy your parents who did not get the opportunity to do so. Another one would be becoming an entrepreneur and taking over the family business. There are literally a million scenarios for this, I am sure you get the picture. Now begin to figure out which ones apply to you.

Now these may be things that you actually want to do for yourself more than anybody else. The key lies in knowing the difference between what you are doing for your personal satisfaction and what you are doing for the satisfaction of the people in your life. It is a thin line with a lot of grey areas. But we must draw the line and be conscious of it, because it is this line which will determine your over all level of satisfaction in life. Ideally, we would love to do both: satisfy ourselves; as well as our loved ones at the same time. Unfortunately, this is not always realistic or reality. Sometimes we have to choose in between the two. While I cannot make the decision for you. It is definitely my pleasure and honor to guide you and inform you so that you can consciously make the best decision that you can live with. In the end it will only be you who knows if you have obtained what your heart desires or if you have sacrificed yourself for the greater good of your loved ones. Both are noble worthy deeds. It is best if we make the most informed intentional decision, rather than deciding overnight without weighing both the pros and cons.

ONE OF ONE

Everyone's current life situation is different. Life is nowhere near a one size fits all type of thing. We all know this, but we do not always act like it. We often times more than not figure if it works for somebody else that it will work for us. While this is true most of the time for most minor things. When it comes to the major things in life, we have to factor in those life circumstances which are unique to us. There is literally only one you on earth. It's great to use the insight others offer you from the outside looking in and you should. They obviously see things that you cannot. On the opposite end you are on the inside, so you know things that are impossible for them to know. Ultimately you are the one who has to live with each decision you make. So you will have to trust yourself more than anyone else when it comes to making these major life decisions.

Personal Advantage

I can guarantee you two things.

1) That you have a specific talent or skill which is far above average when compared to the average human beings' skills in that area. I am not saying that you were innately better, meaning that you came out of the womb better. I am saying that from the moment you were born you excelled with this specific talent or skill in that area faster than the average. Making you sort of an expert or prodigy if you would like to call it that.

2) You have the potential to be among the best in the WORLD when it comes to your specific skill or talent. Being that this skill or talent comes more natural to you than others. It should be common sense to know if it is worked on, perfected, and mastered that you will be among the greatest to ever do whatever it is that you do. We all have the potential to be as great as those we admire. I mean whoever you look at as the greatest in whatever field, you too have that potential to be the greatest in your field. We also all have the opportunity to make a living doing something that we actually love to do, rather than doing something we do not truly love and just tolerate it in order to survive. I believe that is the literal definition of a dream. For life to be an enjoyable experience in which you dominate reality and are ultimately the master of your fate.

REALITY

Now this is not an easy journey or task. I repeat: THIS IS NOT AN EASY JOURNEY OR TASK! If it were easy, EVERYBODY would do it. To live out one's dream is probably the rarest thing that can happen in life EVER. I do not have to use numbers for you to know that the people living out their dreams vs the ones who are not, is a little to a whole lot. Just because you are breathing that does not mean you are living. To truly live is to feel alive more times than not. Your dreams should be so big and scary that they excite you! The fact that your dream can one day become a reality should give you a rush, a burst of energy which helps you do whatever you need to do to make it become reality. If your life is normal right now, then your dreams and goals should sound CRAZY! Just because it may sound crazy does not mean it is not possible. I will give you an example using myself. Me writing this book and you reading it is one of my dreams. If you are reading this right now, then a part of my dream has become true. I put my all into this book in hopes that you can put your all into pursuing your wildest dreams and making them come true as well. I wrote this book during a pandemic, while unemployed, and backed up on bills. Yet I am optimistic and full of hope that this is my way out! This is what I have actually wanted to do for years. Yet like we all do I got sidetracked just surviving and living everyday life. With all this downtime and majority of the world being closed, I am forever grateful to have gotten back to my passion.

Doing what moves me, makes me feel alive, and using my talent to fulfill what I know is my purpose on earth. To communicate and clarify life for the masses.

There is no excuse for a life not lived to the fullest, so please keep rid yourself of all excuses. For even an excuse justified reaps no personal benefit. If you have purchased this book, I hope it truly provides the inspiration, motivation, and clarity you are seeking.

"I owe myself, I told myself back then that I would do this
And It always look so out of reach
And just seem so confusing
Then I found my place in life
A young black man it seems so useless"

- Nipsey Hussle Tha Great

CHAPTER 1:
WHAT IS YOUR PURPOSE?

This is a blessing that you are reading this right now because this means it is not too late. You could be dead right now. The ONLY thing guaranteed in life is death. From the moment you are born and take your first breath, it is 100% guaranteed that you will die one day. Depending on the circumstances some deaths are viewed as negative or positive, either way it just is what it is.

Death has always been a key part of life. We do not know of life without death. Death gives life much more meaning than we often realize. Once we have fully acknowledged that one day we will not exist as we are existing now, we must then ask ourselves, how do we want to be remembered once we are gone?

When we answer that question, we can then begin to critically think about how we must live our lives so that we can be remembered in that way. The things we will have to do, how we must do them, and to the extent they will have to be done. The true details of the matter will come to you once you begin to consistently take action.

Through consistent intentional action it will become clearer and clearer what is working and what is not working. Do not continue to do what is not working for the sake of your pride. As soon as you know that something is not working and taking you in the direction of your goals. You need to stop what you are doing and readjust immediately.

Right next to the fact that death is guaranteed, is the fact that you only live once! This means your one life experience is sacred. Most things in life can be replaced if gone missing or repaired if broken. Two things that can never be replaced or repaired are 1) Your time 2) Your life. While there is room to debate what happens to us when we die, there is a general understanding that we will never return as the same person, in the same skin which we are living in now. Time will not allow it. Time goes forward non-stop, forever, never backwards.

Once we are born the one thing, we are all wealthy in is time. However, you spend your time, is up to you. But once it is spent it is also gone forever. You can never press rewind to redo something differently or to not do it all. While many of us aspire to become wealthy in physical resources, we are all already wealthy in time. We all have the same 24 hours in a day. You decide how you spend your time through your own free will, so of course the results vary. All we have is time, but we do not have unlimited time. Time has us on a strict schedule of always moving forward forever. The past will always remain the past and the future is always up to us. This present moment is what decides what the future will be. Therefore, we must be conscious of the outcome we are seeking before acting. Action is always where the magic happens.

With these three different things in mind - death, life, and limited time - we must come up with 1) a worthy purpose/goals 2) concrete plans to realize this purpose and achieve our goals.
These two focal points will allow us to live up to our full potential. They are what gives us tunnel vision in this journey of life. A decision made with the end goal in mind versus a decision just made in the moment will breed two completely different outcomes. Doing something that will benefit you in the moment can be the exact same thing that will cause you to not accomplish your greatest goal in the long run.

You can only know this by actually knowing your greatest goal and keeping it in the front and the back of your mind during every decision you make. This is why it is chess, not checkers. No two situations are the same, the outcome you seek now must align with the outcome you see in the long run. You must keep your eyes on the prize because every move made changes your position on the board. There is never going to be a "perfect" time to act – so it is best to take action not now, but right now. You will feel better about the outcome of your life knowing that you played a part in favor for yourself.

It's refreshing when you realize YOU are the only thing standing in your way. You have to get out of your own way and realize the only thing holding you back is you, because everything in this world is literally out of your control except yourself. You have to control what you can control which is yourself, your vision, your mood, your thoughts, your feelings, your plans are all up to you.

Testimony: Purpose

I figured out my Purpose when I realize Life was bigger than me. Life is NOT so much of what you can do for yourself but what you can do for others. I knew playing professional basketball was not my purpose because I would only be helping me. I saw that becoming a trainer and lifestyle coach could impact my community which would help the people that are lost on this road called "life".

When I struggled figuring out my purpose the only thing I could look in the mirror and ask myself was "how can I leave a legacy?" "how can I help my people?", and once I meditated on those questions, here I am today as a basketball trainer, lifestyle coach, and voice of the youth. Until this day because of my skill level, People Often ask me why don't I go play basketball professionally. My answer is ALWAYS the same, "God is using me for something greater" (which is my purpose in life)- Kevin Kuteyi (Uncle Skoob).

"Do you have the gift of speaking? Then speak as though God himself were speaking through you. Do you have the gift of helping others? Do it with all the strength and energy that God supplies. Then everything you do will bring glory to God through Jesus Christ. All glory and power to him forever and ever! Amen." {Peter 1:4}

Interactives:

1) How do you want to be remembered once you are no longer living?
2) What purpose do you strongly affiliate with your life with?
3) What is your strongest unique talent?
4) How can you use your talent to further the purpose you have identified with?

CHAPTER 2:
LETTING GO OF OTHERS' EXPECTATIONS

Literally nothing is perfect, and nothing ever will be. There are so many things in life that are literally out of our control that we must accept. The best thing to do is accept these things and focus on the things that we can control. There is not one human being on earth who gets to choose what family they are born into. No one gets to choose when they are born, where they are born, or how they are raised. We are completely powerless in these and countless other aspects of life. However, there is power in realizing this truth.

We all come from a mix of two families, people unique in their culture, traditions, beliefs, and experiences. From the moment we are conceived we are influenced and conditioned by our family's way of living life. The same way our family members were influenced and conditioned before us. For example, we are born into practicing whatever religion our parents' practice. We are not taught about each of the different religions in the world, and then given a chance to decide what we would like to practice. In our infancy we do not have the capacity to even make these types of decisions.

On top of the fact that our parents may not even be aware of other different religion in the world. Whether their parents chose this religion for them or not does not matter. Because it is now being passed down to you without a choice. The same as the things that were involuntary passed down to them.

Reminder this is just one scenario, it may not be religion but we have many things that are decided for us until we have reached the point of making decisions for ourself. Things that have been passed down to us by our families create cycles and these cycles take place in more than just the category of religion. Generation after generation your family can choose to live in the same area of the world without exploring other parts. Or they can choose to take on the same occupation without exploring other careers. For example, you can be born into a family coming from a history of cops, firefighters, or teachers and choose to follow in those footsteps. Your family can have a history of not dating other races, holding onto certain political views, or having hatred towards a group of people for whatever reason.

Regardless, if you choose to accept things passed down to you or you reject them, you have to separate yourself in knowing your real reason for doing so. Separating yourself from others who simply do things for reasons that are not their own will take you to another level of life.

As we grow older, we begin to have our own life experiences from which we can draw our own conclusions from. Until you are of a certain age you are pretty much being guided by the conclusions that your guardians have made from their experiences. Things that were once extremely true for them and their generation, may now be extinct to you.

Once we have grown and matured to a certain point, we have the power in deciding which generational cycles we will break, which we may uphold, and why. These are all personal decisions which should be influenced most by personal experiences. You must separate yourself from others' expectations on your life. It does not matter who "they" are. You should not live your ENTIRE life trying to live up to others' expectations because you may never reach their expectations. On top of that their satisfaction does not equal your satisfaction, just as yours does not equal theirs.

But you can always meet your own realistic expectations. You must consciously reject other expectations which do not align with the purpose you have conceived for your life. This is not emotionally easy, and you may receive backlash from your family for living your life in a way that may not make sense to them. However, this must be done for the simple fact that you can be successful in everyone else's eyes and a failure in your own if you are not truly happy.

This is your life, no one knows how your shoes fit and feel better than you. You are the one that has to die when it's time for you to die. So please live your life the way you decide to because it is time to live free of the burden of other expectations! Live a life that works for you. It is not anyone's responsibility to know you more than you know yourself, and it is actually impossible for them to do so.

Most people will never genuinely imagine what it is like to walk in your shoes. So, any advice or opinion is literally limited to their external outlook of you and your life. So, most might not ever understand why you do what you do, but know it is not their place to understand. Even if you were hypothetically doing it for them.

The flip side of this is still hearing out the people who have your best interest at heart. Most people in life will simply use you for what they can get from you, period. However, there is a small group of people who truly care about you even when they do not get anything out of the deal. You must cherish these people and always consider the perspective and opinions that they offer you. They only want the best for you, everything they do is out of love. The other group of people who are simply trying to use you as a means to an end are the ones you must be extremely cautious of. Everything they do is for the advancement of their own objectives; they could honestly care less what happens to you.

Testimony: Letting Go

Basketball is my life & I love it with everything in me, but I was so blind to realizing that—that was not my purpose in life. I was too scared to transition into anything else because I felt I would be a failure in the eyes of others. I never wanted to be viewed as someone who gives up. Everyone, and I mean everyone, knew me for playing basketball and expected me to go pro, so I never wanted to stop chasing that dream. But if I chose to live my life based on how others would have perceived me, you probably would not even be reading this book!

-Kevin Kuteyi (Uncle Skoob)

"And you will know the truth, and the truth will set you free." {John 8:32}

Interactives:
1) At this exact point in your life what do you feel like or know is expected from you by others?
2) At this point in your life, what expectations do you have for yourself that no one else may be aware about?
3) Between these two groups of expectations, please detail out which expectations align. Which expectations that others have for you as well as the ones you have for yourself. These are the expectations that you should be striving towards moving forward.

CHAPTER 3: BRAINSTOMRING WITHOUT LIMITS

To truly know better is to do better, there is no in between with this. If you are not doing better than what you are now it is because you do not know any better. So, we must know ourselves better to demand better for ourselves. We must shed the skin of trying to live up to other people's expectations of how we should live our lives. We must realize our own passion and goals and strive for them. When we do not truly know ourselves and we're constantly being influenced by others, it is impossible to be our authentic selves.

When we conceive an authentic purpose for our lives, one we can feel comfortable dedicating our lives too. Only then can we begin to do better for ourselves without the need for outside confirmations. Outside confirmations are useful and definitely do come in handy when in doubt, but they are always secondary, and they should never be primary. Worst case scenario outside confirmations can lead you to your demise, because internally you are still lost. You yourself must be sure before anyone else can be sure of you.

Let us remove the thought of outside judgement and brainstorm without limits for a second. This may even be your first time doing this which is awesome. I want you to imagine how you would dream to live your life if you did not have to hear the opinions and judgements from your loved ones. Really imagine deeply. This purpose must be fulfilling to you first and foremost, then you can begin considering other people.

We are all a part of the bigger picture, but we must not exclude ourselves. Logic and heart go hand in hand, never one without the other. The same with passion and purpose, you must be passionate about something you constantly choose to engage in. There is a major difference in the things we have to do sometimes versus the things that we simply choose to do all the time

Balance is key, action is the rhythm of life. Let the fresh thoughts come in, as you release the burden of trying to live up to the expectations of you from others. Remove the limits and realize that they were set in place for the comfort of other people. Create a new solid vision which is ideal, unique, and specific to your wants and needs. How do you see yourself making the rest of your life the best of your life? How sad would it be to live up to everyone else's expectations and not our own.

Testimony: Brainstorming

You need time to yourself to really focus on you. Once I figured out that being a pro basketball player was not what God wanted for me, I started to brainstorm and think about how I could add value to my community while doing something I love. Clearly, I love basketball. So I thought – why not teach it to kids? I would be able to do what I loved each day, while teaching valuable lessons to the next generation. I decided to start with my nephews which led into other small wins.

-Kevin Kuteyi (Uncle Skoob)

"So let it grow, for when your endurance is fully developed, you will be perfect and complete, needing nothing." {James 1:4}

Interactives:

1) What is something you love to do so passionately that you would do it even if you were not getting paid for it?
2) How can you use this thing that you are passionate about to make a positive impact in the world and on how you are remembered?
3) What are some things that you find yourself doing just to continue to live up to the expectation's others? How are these things affecting you? Do you honestly want to continue you doing these things or do you wish to stop as soon as possible?

CHAPTER 4:
SMALL WINS

You give life a new meaning when you start dreaming, and when you stop dreaming is when you start dying. After you have the answers to these questions it is time to start taking steps to living the life that you want for yourself and not just the life that others want for you. There will be points where your life aligns where you are living for yourself and others simultaneously. This is the beauty of life this is where you are truly living out your purpose and using your unique talents to add value to the world.

We should all aim to be the best in the world at what we do. If you have not aimed too high, then you have definitely aimed to low. Becoming the best at what you do increases the odds significantly on you having a powerful impact in the world. These are two of the greatest aspirations one can have in life. But since we are in the process of truly figuring out how we want to live our lives and what we would like to accomplish we must focus on the small wins. During the initial transition of beginning this new journey it is best for us to focus on the small wins. Those small wins will eventually lead to that big win.

Tracking your progress by small wins is the most effective mental tool you can use to make sure you are always one step closer to achieving your goals and fulfilling your purpose. One of the most mind-blowing truths that you can realize is that you are a real-life prophet, and your life is your testimony. It is the truth of the passion in your heart and the proof of your purpose in existence.

You cannot take the path of least resistance if you are to be a master of your fate. You must control what you can control to increase the odds. Delay does not equal defeat, consistently investing in small wins will consistently bring you closer to accomplishing your greatest goal. Begin as small as possible with your eyes on the prize. If your goal is to start your own business, the first logical step of course would be to get your LLC. That right there is a small win! That is a step that brings you closer to your overall goal. You see...it is best we break it down step by step and focus on each step once we have already imagined our overall goal. The journey of a thousand steps starts with one step, and regardless of how it seems no one step is more important then the other. Since all steps are required to make it to the promise land.

Testimony: Small Wins

Everyday counts. Training my nephews just 3x a week gave me momentum, which led me to pick up another client – another small win. I worked the Nike summer camp with former WNBA guard Sonia Chase and I saw potential in Tiana Jackson so I exchanged info with her mom. Tiana is special because she is my first committed paying client, and while I wasn't compensated for training my nephew, those sessions gave and continue to give me confidence to offer my services. The point is, if you don't work on your craft and focus on small wins, you'll never truly be ready for that big win.

-Kevin Kuteyi (Uncle Skoob)

"Do not despise these small beginnings, for the Lord rejoices to see the work begin." {Zechariah 4:10}

Interactives:

1) What are your greatest goals? Business or personal. When it is all said and done what impact do you want to have had on the world, your community, and the people in your life?
2) What is the first step towards accomplishing that goal? How about the next two? I want you to be as detailed as possible.
3) What are some other small wins that you can think of that will put you closer to your purpose and long-term goals? I want you to think as small as possible. This is a long journey and no matter how irrelevant it may seem, I want you to name it because everything counts!

CHAPTER 5: SACRIFICE

If you want something bad enough you will find a way. But you can never get something for nothing. Nothing in this life is ever free - we are always paying for life in a combination of time, resources, and energy. We all breathe the same air, sleep the same sleep, and bleed the same blood. Yet there are those of us who can manifest reality, accomplish our goals, and make our dreams come true.

As well as those who are not able to meet their mark, have the impact they wish for themselves or accomplish the goals set for themselves. We must ask our self what are the fundamental differences between the two? The answer is simple. Sacrifices. To whom much is given much is tested and to accomplish great things great sacrifices must be made. How you spend your time, resources, and energy will ultimately decide if you are successful in the journey of life.

Sacrifices must be made. Small wins will require small sacrifices, as you move on to bigger wins, they will require greater sacrifices. You must first assess the price of each goal or aspiration and decide if the price is worth paying. Anything is possible, but again it is never free of charge. Success is expensive so you must budget your life accordingly. Never deceive yourself regarding what you are willing to sacrifice to accomplish your goals. You must be honest in what you are willing to do and what you are not. Once you have an idea of the price of success, you can begin working and investing the right amount of time, resources and energy until your mark is met.

We are living in a society where we have access to each other's lives more than ever. 10-20 years ago, we did not know where everyone worked, what they drove, how much money they have, and what they do in their spare time. These days we have people we have kept up with for years who we have not seen in real life one time! Its kind of crazy when you put it like that. I say that to say this, in this day and age we see things and just want them. When in reality we think we want them until we find out what they cost.

I am not just talking about money here. Everything cost more than money, it is time, hard work, blood, sweat, tears etc. You pay for what you get with what you can no longer have. We have to be conscious of what we truly want in the long run vs what we simply desire in the moment. We must sacrifice for the greater good of ourselves if we are to ever reach our true goals. We cannot have everything all at once right now. It is impossible.

Testimony: Sacrifice

I deleted all my social media accounts for a whole year so I could focus solely on me only. I sacrificed time with friends, and I eliminated almost all fun. I was dedicated to my craft and I can definitely say it was worth it because those friends are still my friends today and social media did not go anywhere. Consistency is really key no matter how cliche it sounds. You have to treat your dreams like a plant. There is no way it will grow if you do not water it. If you water it for 1 week, it will grow but then it will die if you stop for one week. Each time you stop you set yourself back.

-Kevin Kuteyi (Uncle Skoob)

"He gave his life to purchase freedom for everyone. This is the message God gave to the world at just the right time."

{Timothy 2:6}

Interactives:

1) What are the sacrifices that are going to have to be made so that you are able to live the life that you want? Think about time, money, and your current resources. These are your greatest assets.

2) What sacrifices are you not willing to make for whatever reason? Be realistic. Some things are too compromising and not worth it in the long run. Being aware of this will allow you to find another way.

CHAPTER 6:
DISCIPLINE

Everything you have just read does not matter if you do not have discipline! Discipline is the key that opens the doors to all opportunities. There is literally no limit to all that one can accomplish once a solid discipline has been established. On the other hand, you will literally not be able to accomplish anything lasting or worthy without some form of discipline.

The difference between consistency and a coincidence is discipline. It is not about what you do sometimes it is about what you do all the time on a consistent basis. Discipline is what turns consistency into momentum, allowing you to get better faster than others who continuously start and stop. When you are about to stop you need to remember why you started, as cliché as it sounds. Because when you stop you are not getting better! When you push through and stick to the script even when you do not feel like it, you grow and become better.

We all know hard work beats talent when talent does not work hard. I take it even further to say no talent at all and a strong discipline is better than all talent and no discipline. Discipline has nothing to do with talent, it has everything to do with WILL POWER. We all have will power and must exercise it for it to become stronger, will power is the force that you must put behind your talent or skill to propel it and take it to another level.

There is no compromise or work around that can be taken in regard to building discipline.

It must be built and maintained day in day out until it becomes a strong habit which is then easier to maintain. Start right now with what you have because what you have is plenty. You literally have everything you need right now to make your dreams come true, by accomplishing short term goals now and long-term goals in the future. Discipline is what allows you to ration off the proper amount of time, energy, and resources on a consistent basis. This will bring about compound interest through consistency. Allowing you to maximize your full potential, by reaching levels that could not be reaching starting and stopping.

Testimony: Discipline

When I deleted my social media and separated myself from almost everything besides my immediate family, it required serious discipline. It's easy to look in the mirror and say you will or won't do something because you are most likely high in the moment, but when the time actually comes and you feel like doing what you said you wouldn't do, that's when you activate Discipline! There were times my friends would call me and text me asking to hang out with them. As much as I would want to sometimes, just for a relief of being by myself. I had to stay disciplined and remain locked in on my goals.I was busy finding myself and activating my authentic self. It was a MUST that I stay disciplined and practice delayed gratification.

-Kevin Kuteyi (Uncle Skoob)

"No discipline is enjoyable while it is happening--- it is painful! But there will be a peaceful harvest for those who are trained this way." {Hebrews 12}

Interactives:

1) What consistent action do you need to be disciplined in taking consistently in order to gain small wins on the regular?
2) What activities are counterproductive and need to be refrained from consistently? Be completely honest with yourself here. There are things which only you know you part take in; others cannot offer this advice because they do not know of these activities.
3) How can you track your growth and progress in areas you are building discipline in? You must measure your small wins consistently as well, they will let you know exactly how far you are coming along and how much closer you are to that big win.

OUTRO

Congratulations for making to the end of the book! We thank you for your continuous support. We really hope this book has helped you at least take one step closer to your purpose in life. The best has yet to come, trust me when I say this. THE BEST HAS YET TO COME! Use this book as a guide and refer back to it whenever needed.

Made in the USA
Middletown, DE
16 May 2022

65848713R00027